Poetry *from the* Masters

THE BLACK ARTS MOVEMENT

D1552571

An Introduction to African-American Poets
Edited by Useni Eugene Perkins

For information regarding permission, write to:
Just Us Books, Inc.
356 Glenwood Avenue
East Orange, NJ 07017
www.justusbooks.com

Printed in the USA
12 11 10 9 8 7 6 5 4 3 2 1
Library of Congress Cataloging-in-publication data is available.

ISBN
1-978-933491-13-2

Cover illustration copyright 2009 by Stephan J. Hudson.
Acknowledgments for poems appear at the end of the book.

Dedicated in memory of Ruwa Chiri,
Sigmonde Wimberly and Cynthia Conley—poets who
also contributed to the Black Arts Movement.

Contents

Foreword

A Changing of the Conversation

*D*eep knowledge of one's culture is an absolute necessity, especially as we attempt to navigate our lives in an ever-evolving world. Any people who are anchored in their own cultural imperatives—visual art, literature, history, science, music, religion, politics, and economics—surely will walk more confidently than people with little or negative knowledge of themselves. Critical self-knowledge starts with an introduction to the best that a culture has to offer.

The Black Arts Movement artists and writers clearly hit the ground running in the United States around 1965 and influenced poets, writers, and artists worldwide. BAM poets carried a message of Black cultural, psychological, and economic liberation that had not been heard since the Harlem Renaissance of the 1920s and 1930s. The Black poetry created between 1965 and 1975 introduced a Black Aesthetic that did not compromise its essential reasons for existence: Black liberation, redefinition, and empowerment. Useni Eugene Perkins, a formidable poet-playwright of the Black Arts Movement (BAM), has edited a collection of poetry that introduces the founding creators of the vibrant and essential poetry of the 1960s and 1970s to a new audience.

During the highly political, dangerous and defining decades of the 1960s and 1970s, America experienced two wars: one fought in Viet Nam and the other found in America's urban communities and in its universities. On university campuses across the country, Black literature punctured holes in its perceived literary canon as its legions of gatekeepers tried desperately to destroy the existence of any literature outside of its well-defined perimeters. In other words, if White men didn't write, publish, teach, and analyze it, it (Black, feminist, and others) did not exist.

The value of this collection, *Poetry from the Masters: The Black Arts Movement*, is in keeping with the underlying meaning of the Black Arts Movement. This volume clearly builds upon the premise that self-definition leads to critical self-awareness, which generally stimulates decisive action when confronting political, economic disparities and especially when confronting historically negative images of Black people.

It was during the turbulent 1960s when young Americans stood up against an unjust war. It was during the 1960s when Black people ceased being "Negroes." Most of us began to define ourselves as Black people, people of African ancestry, i.e., African Americans. Black to us was not only color, but also culture and consciousness. We changed the conversation and it was the poets and artists of our communities who took the lead in redefining Black existence in America and the world. Maulena Karenga, Hoyt W. Fuller, Larry Neal, Eugenia Collier, Stephen E. Henderson, Addison Gayle Jr., John O. Killens, and others worked diligently inside and outside of the academy to develop an intellectual construct for the future study of this important decade and its cultural workers.

A major consideration for the importance of this collection is that it introduces to young readers the best of BAM poets just as revisionist "scholars" try to reduce the influence of BAM literature to a mere footnote. Professor Perkins and Just Us Books have rendered a huge service to the reading public.

Our continued challenge is to aid in the development of a literate, whole, well-informed, and empowered citizen who will question everything. Remember, they who build roads also define the steps and direction taken on the road. The BAM poets went off-road—designed and crafted in their poetry, new highways. They laid the foundation for today's rap, hip-hop, and spoken-word artists. Many of them also created independent Black institutions and continue to this day to fight against a leadership bent on keeping us ignorant and dependent. This collection represents one confirmation of our literary history that helped to change this country for the best and continues to challenge corporate and popular culture.

Haki Madhubuti
Poet, Publisher of Third World Press
University Distinguished Professor
and Director of the MFA Program
in Creative Writing at Chicago State University

Overview

The Black Arts Movement

espite the end of the Harlem Renaissance in the late 1930s, Black poets continued to create important works of art. Among these poets were Arna Bontemps, Langston Hughes, Sterling Brown, Margaret A. Walker, Melvin B. Tolson, Margaret Danner, Frank Marshall Davis, Robert E. Hayden and Gwendolyn Brooks. These talented poets preserved the African-American poetic tradition, but they did not always share a common ideology that would identify a particular trend or style. Instead, their poetry reflected a wide range of themes and artistic expressions.

During the early 1960s, however, a new thrust in the arts was being expressed and it began a new era for aspiring Black poets. This thrust of Black creativity blossomed with the emergence of new Black organizations that departed from the ideology of traditional civil rights organizations. Among these new organizations were the Black Panther Party, co-founded by Bobby Seale and Huey P. Newton in 1966; the Black Liberation Front founded in 1966; the Republic of New Afrika, founded in 1969; and the U.S. Organization, founded by Dr. Maulana Karenga, who also created Kwanzaa in 1966. Although traditional civil rights organizations such as the National Association for the Advancement of Colored People, National Urban League, Congress of Racial Equality and the Southern Christian Leadership Conference led by Dr. Martin Luther King, Jr. continued to lead the Civil Rights Movement, their leadership was being challenged by many of these new organizations. This challenge took on great significance when Stokely Carmichael, leader of the Student Non-Violent Coordinating Committee, called for Black Power in 1966 and many of these groups responded to his message. Many of the new poets were attracted to the concept of Black Power, which became a central theme in the Black Arts Movement. Larry Neal, poet and a leading voice in the Black Arts Movement, made the following statement about this relationship to Black Power:

"The Black Arts Movement is radically opposed to any concept of the artist that alienates him from his community. Black Art is the aesthetic and spiritual sister of the Black Power concept. As such, it envisions an art that speaks directly to the needs and aspirations of Black America."

Also during the 1960s, Black students at colleges and universities across America demanded more Black faculty members and Black studies courses. There were sit-ins, marches, and demonstrations throughout the nation. Urban unrest plagued many American cities. Many Blacks lost their lives during this period in their efforts to remind White America that it had not yet atoned for centuries of legalized slavery and oppression of Black people. The Black Arts Movement must be understood in this context to appreciate the Black artists who challenged America to be true to its doctrine of freedom and justice for all of its citizens.

Not since the Harlem Renaissance had Black artists received so much attention as they did during this period. But unlike the Harlem Renaissance, which was, in part, financed by White patrons of the arts, the Black Arts

Movement was rooted in Black nationalism, self-reliance and self-determination. Throughout America, Black artists were challenging the traditional European interpretation of art and were more concerned with creating art that was relevant to the Black community. James T. Stewart, a poet and critic, affirmed this challenge when he wrote:

> "The dilemma of the Negro artist is that he makes assumptions based on the wrong models. He makes assumptions based on white models. These assumptions are not only wrong, they are antithetical to our existence. The Black artist must construct models which correspond to his own reality. The models must be non-white. Our models must be consistent with Black lifestyle, our aesthetic and our moral and spiritual styles."

Historically, Black artists had been forced to adopt to European and Western standards and traditions in order to have their work accepted. Almost all Black art was judged against this model and the art that dared to be different was denounced as inferior and not authentic. Some defenders of the Western tradition even questioned whether it was viable for Black artists to draw from the Black experiece and Black culture for their subject matter. But these critics deliberately dismissed or failed to recognize a heritage that dates back to ancient Egypt, the world's oldest civilization and the legacy, struggle and achievement of Blacks in America. In their refusal to accept these criticisms, Black poets celebrated Black life and were critical of those who tried to degrade their work.

While Black poets were generally seen as the most vocal advocates of the Black Arts Movement, musicians, dramatists, dancers, visual artists and other Black artists were a part of this movement as well. Indeed, the Black Arts Movement represented many aspects of Black culture and allowed Black artists to freely express themselves as they had never done before.

Black publishing companies played significant roles in promoting the works of Black poets. Third World Press in

Chicago, Broadside Press in Detroit, and literary journals and magazines such as the *Journal of Black Poetry*, *Black Books Bulletin*, *Black Dialogue*, *Freedomways* and *Black Scholar* provided outlets for poets hungry to get their poetry published. The publication that gave many poets that opportunity was *Negro Digest*, later to be renamed *Black World*. Headed by editor Hoyt Fuller, *Black World* was committed to publishing new writers and provided a national audience for their work. It also helped to pave the way for Black literary seminars, college forums and writers conferences that helped to expand the scope of the Black Arts Movement.

Today, many Black cultural institutions can trace their roots to the Black Arts Movement. Theaters, museums, film companies, art galleries and other cultural institutions— even songs such as Nina Simone's "To Be Young Gifted and Black" and James Brown's "I'm Black and I'm Proud" can be considered a part of the movement.

The poets of the Black Arts Movement used various techniques and styles to express themselves, but they all shared a passion to make their poetry creditable and descriptive of the Black experience. Common among many of these poets was the use of the "language of the streets," including rappin', signifying and "Black English" to communicate more directly to the masses of Black people. This enabled their poetry to reach a broader and more diverse number of Black people who normally were not necessarily impressed with traditional poetry. Just like today's hip hop poets, poets of the Black Arts Movement would read their poetry in a variety of places, on street corners, in parks and other places where Black people would congregate. The unique rhythms and cadences of the Last Poets, Haki Madhubuti, Sonia Sanchez and Nikki Giovanni still influence hip hop today.

The Black poets who are profiled in this book represent many, but not all, of the poets who made a significant contribution to the Black Arts Movement. Poets who are not included but were also important participants include A.B. Spellman, Audre Lorde, Henry Dumas, Marvin X, Ishmael Reed, Bob Kaufman and Ted Joans.

Even though some of the poets included in this book no longer confine their poetry to the ideology that defined the Black Arts Movement, few would deny that that ideology was crucial to their artistic development.

Useni Eugene Perkins

Amiri Baraka

b. 1933
Political and Cultural Sage

Amiri Baraka, whose birth name is Leroi Jones, has been acclaimed by many advocates of the Black Arts Movement as its most charismatic, political and cultural sage. This recognition is given to him because of the major role he played in helping to define and give direction to the movement. Through his writing and activism, Baraka expressed Black Arts ideology. His prose, plays and poetry became models for other to emulate.

Born in 1933 in Newark, New Jersey, Baraka attended Rutgers University, Howard University and Columbia University. He also served in the U.S. Air Force from 1954 to 1957. His early writing, although rooted in African-American culture, was more influenced by the literary trends that were being developed by White avant garde poets who lived primarily in New York's Greenwich Village. There he met Allen Ginsberg, Frank O'Hara and Gilbert Sorrentino, who were exploring new and different literary styles. After a trip to Cuba in 1960, however, where he was influenced by so-called Third World artists, Baraka's writing became more political. Greenwich Village had lost its appeal when he returned from Cuba. After receiving national acclaim for his first volume of poetry, *Preface to a Twenty Volume Suicide Note* in 1963, he moved to Harlem, New York, where he became a leader in the Black arts community. Many scholars credit him with coining the name Black Art.

Following the death of Malcolm X in 1964, Baraka helped to found the Black Arts Repertory Theater (BART), which became one of the leading Black cultural institutions in America. BART attracted prominent writers such as Larry Neal, Askia Muhammad Toure, Marvin X and musicians such as Archie Shepp, Eric Dolphy and Sun Ra. Later Baraka opened Spirit House and Jihad Productions in his hometown of Newark, New Jersey. Both institutions promoted Black nationalism through cultural rituals, music and theater.

In 1968, along with Larry Neal, Baraka edited *Black Fire, An Anthology of Afro-American Writing*, a book that introduced the works of many poets of the Black Arts Movement. Throughout the period, Baraka produced important works, including the collections *Black Magic* (1967), *Black Art, Collected Poetry* (1969), and the plays *Slave Ship* (1967), *Great Goodness of Life* (1967), and *Arm Yourself or Harm Yourself* (1967).

For a brief period Baraka abandoned Black Nationalism when he became attracted to social Maxism as a way to address the plight of Black people. But his experience in social Maxism was short-lived and he resumed his leadership role in the Black Arts Movement. Among many of his major awards and honors include a John Whitney Foundation Award (1962), an honorary doctorate from Malcolm X University in Chicago (1962), the New Jersey Council for the Arts Award (1982), the American Book Award (1984), and the National Endowment for the Arts Poetry Award (1981). In 1998, he was inducted into the International Literary Hall of Fame for Writers of African Descent by the Gwendolyn Brooks Center at Chicago State University.

Some critics claim that Amiri Baraka compromised his literary talent to promote his political views. None, however, can deny his status as a major literary figure in the United States and in the world.

Preface to a Twenty Volume Suicide Note

For Kellie Jones, born 16 May 1959

Lately, I've become accustomed to the way
The ground opens up and envelopes me
Each time I go out to walk the dog.
Or the broad edged silly music the wind
Makes when I run for a bus . . .

Things have come to that.

And now, each night I count the stars,
And each night I get the same number.
And when they will not come to be counted,
I count the holes they leave.

Nobody sings anymore.

And then last night, I tiptoed up
To my daughter's room and heard her
Talking to someone, and when I opened
The door, there was no one there . . .
Only she on her knees, peeking into

Her own clasped hands.

Amiri Baraka

Ka 'Ba

A closed window looks down
on a dirty courtyard, and black people
call across or scream or walk across
defying physics in the stream of their will

Our world is full of sound
Our world is more lovely than anyone's
tho we suffer, and kill each other
and sometimes fail to walk the air

We are beautiful people
with african imaginations
full of masks and dances and swelling chants

with african eyes, and noses, and arms,
though we sprawl in grey chains in a place
full of winters, when what we want is sun.

We have been captured,
brothers. And we labor
to make our getaway, into
the ancient image, into a new

correspondence with ourselves
and our black family. We need magic
now we need the spells, to rise up
return, destroy, and create. What will be

the sacred words?

A Poem for Black Hearts

For Malcolm's eyes, when they broke
the face of some dumb white man, For
Malcolm's hands raised to bless us
all black and strong in his image
of ourselves, for Malcolm's words
fire darts, the victor's tireless
thrusts, words hung above the world
change as it may, he said it, and
for this he was killed, for saying,
and feeling, and being / change, all
collected hot in his heart, For Malcolm's
heart, raising us above our filthy cities,
for his stride, and his beat, and his address
to the grey monsters of the world, For Malcolm's
pleas for your dignity, black men, for your life,
black man, for the filling of your minds
with righteousness, For all of him dead and
gone and vanished from us, and all of him which
clings to our speech black god of our time.
For all of him, and all of yourself, look up,
black man, quit stuttering and shuffling, look up,
black man, quit whining and stooping, for all of him,
For Great Malcolm a prince of the earth, let nothing
    in us rest
until we avenge ourselves for his death, stupid animals
that killed him, let us never breathe a pure breath if
we fail, and white men call us faggots till the end of
the earth.

Amiri Baraka   **5**

Mari Evans

b. 1923

Trailblazer

When the Black Arts Movement began in the mid-sixties, Mari Evans had already established herself as a prominent literary figure. Several of her poems were included in the historical collection *Dark Symphony, Negro Literature In America* (1968), edited by James A. Emanuel and Theodore L. Gross. Unlike some Black poets of her generation who were slow to embrace the movement, Evans became one of its most revered mentors. Her commitment to social change prior to the beginning of the Black Arts Movement informed her role as a cultural activist. In her book of essays *Clarity As Concept, A Poet's Perspective*, Evans writes:

> *"I would argue, however, that a more significant development has been the manner in which writers continue to innovate; to hone and focus their creativity in ways that are obvious musical replications, as they present in new works material rich with craft that evolved from the innovative Black Arts Movement."*

Fellow writer and friend Maya Angelou has said "Evans is a sharp observer and an honest person." This honesty is succintly and powerfully demonstrated in her famous poem, "Speak The Truth To The People."

Evans was born in Toledo, Ohio in 1923, but has spent most of her life in Indianapolis, Indiana. Her first volume of poetry, *Where Is All The Music?* was published in 1968. That same year she received a Woodrow Wilson grant and in 1969 began the first of many appointments teaching at American colleges and universities. She has taught at Cornell University where she was Distinguished Writer and Assistant Professor, African American Resource Center, Indiana University, the State University of New York at Albany and Spelman College.

Other volumes of poetry Evans has authored include *I Am A Black Woman* (1970), *Night Star* (1981) and *A Dark & Splendid Mass* (1992). One of her most important works is a book she edited, *Black Women Writers (1950–1980): A Critical Evaluation* (1984). The collection has become a major resource for those studying the works of Black women writers.

Multi-talented, in addition to poetry, Evans has written prose, musicals, plays and children's literature. Her books for children include *I Look At Me* (1973), *JD* (1973), *Singing Black* (1976 and 2004), *Jim Flying High* (1979) and *I'm Late* (2006). Among her dramas are *Rivers of My Song* (1977), *Portrait of a Man* and *Moochie* (both in 1979) and *Eyes* (1979), an adaptation of Zora Neale Hurston's gripping novel of southern life, *Their Eyes Were Watching God*. *My Father's Passage*, a book of autobiographical essays, was published in 1984.

Evans has received many awards and honors, including a John Hay Whitney Fellowship (1975), Alaine Locke/Gwendolyn Brooks Award for Excellence in Literature (1995), induction into Chicago State University's International Literary Hall of Fame for Writers of African Descent (1998), and an honorary doctorate degree from Martin University (1999). She was also honored by Uganda with her photo on a postage stamp.

Evans continues to live in Indianapolis, Indiana, where she still writes, lectures and is active in community and national causes.

Speak Truth to the People

Speak truth to the people
Talk sense to the people
Free them with honesty
Free the people with Love and Courage for their Being
Spare them the fantasy
Fantasy enslaves
A slave is enslaved
Can be enslaved by unwisdom
Can be re-enslaved while in flight from the enemy
Can be enslaved by his brother whom he loves
His brother whom he trusts whom he loves
His brother whom he trusts
His brother with the loud voice
And the unwisdom
Speak the truth to the people
It is not necessary to green the heart
Only to identify the enemy
It is not necessary to blow the mind
Only to free the mind
To identify the enemy is to free the mind
A free mind has no need to scream

A free mind is ready for other things

To BUILD black schools
To BUILD black children
To BUILD black minds
To BUILD black love
To BUILD black impregnability
To BUILD a strong black nation
To BUILD

Speak the truth to the people
Spare them the opium of devil-hate
They need no trips on honky-chants.

Move them instead to a BLACK ONENESS.

A black strength which will defend its own
Needing no cacophony of screams for activation
A black strength which will attack the laws
exposes the lies, disassembles the structure
and ravages the very foundation of evil.
Speak the truth to the people
To identify the enemy is to free the mind
Free the mind of the people
Speak to the mind of the people
Speak Truth

I Am A Black Woman

I am a black woman
the music of my song
some sweet arpeggio of tears
is written in a minor key
and I
can be heard humming in the night
Can be heard
          humming
in the night

I saw my mate leap screaming to the sea
and I/with these hands/cupped the lifebreath
from my issue in the canebreak
I lost Nat's swinging body in a rain of tears
and heard my son scream all the way from Anzio
for Peace he never knew I
learned Do Nang and Pork Chop Hill
in anguish
Now my nostrils know the gas
and these trigger tire/d fingers
seek the softness in my warrior's beard

I
am a black woman
tall as a cypress
strong
beyond all definition still
defying place
and time
and circumstance

     assailed
        impervious
           indestructible
Look
 on me and be
renewed

Ode to My Sons

I am the vessel from whence you came
the lode filled with imaginings
aside from dreams my longing cannot
touch your reaching nor can I direct
your quest
    Your center is the earth the
cool continuum of mountain stream
the blasting winds
Nor can I follow there for I
am but bound flesh from whence you came
My private-griefs are private griefs
and you will have your fill of such
I wish you joy-and love and strength
a centering of mind and will
a homeward journey to your core
and when chaotic winds subside

an overflow of peace
    a quiet soul

Mari Evans

Nikki Giovanni
b. 1943
Bright and Shining Star

Nikki Giovanni emerged from the Black Arts Movement as one of Black America's brightest stars. While the popularity of many Black poets waned, Giovanni's stature as a poet, activist and feminist grew. Today, she is considered an icon and is perhaps just as popular as she was during the Black Arts Movement.

Giovanni was born in 1943 in Knoxville, Tennessee and spent her childhood years in Cincinnati, Ohio. She first attended Fisk University in 1961 but was suspended because of her rebelliousness. She entered Fisk again in 1964 and graduated in 1967 with a degree in history. While at Fisk she was editor of *Elan*, a literary journal, and was a leader of the Fisk chapter of the Student Nonviolent Coordinating Committee, a national, student-led civil rights organization. While a student, Giovanni became interested in writing. At the first Black Writers' Conference at Fisk in 1966 she met Black writers such as John Oliver Killens, Margaret Walker, Robert Hayden, Dudley Randall, Melvin

Tolson and Amiri Baraka. A second conference was held in 1967. The conferences helped to define Black art and articulate the necessity of Black arts in the struggle for freedom.

Giovanni's first book of poetry, *Black Feeling, Black Talk*, was self-published in 1968. Her second self-published book, *Black Judgement* soon followed. These two volumes established her as an important voice in the Black Arts community. In 1969, the *Amsterdam News* named her "one of the ten most admired Black women" in America. The *New York Times* featured her in an article entitled "Renaissance in Black Poetry Expresses Anger." In 1970, she edited and published *Night Comes Softly*, one of the earliest anthologies of poetry by Black women. That same year William Morrow published *Black Feeling, Black Talk* and *Black Judgement* as one volume and Broadside Press published *Re-Creation. Ebony* magazine named the prolific writer "Woman of the Year" for 1970.

In 1971, Giovanni published her autobiography, *Gemini*, and a volume of poems for children, *Spin A Soft Black Song*. She also released the spoken-word album, *Truth is On the Way*, featuring the New York Community Choir. The album sold more than 100,000 copies in six months.

During her long, outstanding career, Giovanni has written more than 30 fiction and nonfiction books, including eight for children. She has also released nine spoken-word records, tapes and CDs.

In recognition of her outstanding work and contributions, Giovanni has received numerous awards and honors, including nearly 20 honorary doctorate degrees from institutions such as Wilberforce University, Ripon University, the University of Maryland and Smith College. In 1999, she was inducted into the International Literary Hall of Fame for Writers of African Descent and she received a Certificate of Commendation from the U.S. Senate in 2000. Giovanni continues to add to her literary legacy. She is currently a University Distinguished Professor at Virginia Tech in Blacksburg, Virginia.

Ego Tripping (there may be a reason why)

I was born in the congo
I walked to the fertile crescent and built the sphinx
I designed a pyramid so tough that a star
       that only glows every one hundred years falls
       into the center giving divine perfect light
I am bad

I sat on the throne
       drinking nectar with allah
I got hot and sent an ice age to europe
       to cool my thirst
My oldest daughter is nefertiti
       the tears from my birth pains
       created the nile
I am a beautiful woman

I gazed on the forest and burned
       out the sahara desert
       with a packet of goat's meat
       and a change of clothes
I crossed it in two hours
I am a gazelle so swift
       so swift you can't catch me

       For a birthday present when he was three
I gave my son hannibal an elephant
       He gave me rome for mother's day
My strength flows ever on

My son noah built new/ark and
I stood proudly at the helm
       as we sailed on a soft summer day

I turned myself into myself and was
    jesus
        men intone my loving name
        All praises All praises
I am the one who would save

I sowed diamonds in my back yard
My bowels deliver uranium
        the filings from my fingernails are
        semi-precious jewels
        On a trip north
I caught a cold and blew
My nose giving oil to the arab world
I am so hip even my errors are correct
I sailed west to reach east and had to round off
        the earth as I went
        The hair from my head thinned and gold was laid
        across three continents

I am so perfect so divine so ethereal so surreal
I cannot be comprehended except by my permission

I mean . . . I . . . can fly
        like a bird in the sky . . .

Nikki Giovanni   **15**

Knoxville, Tennessee

I always like summer
best
you can eat fresh corn
from daddy's garden
and okra
and greens
and cabbage
and lots of
barbeque
and buttermilk
and homemade ice-cream
at the church picnic
and listen to
gospel music
outside
at the church
homecoming
and go to the mountains with
your grandmother
and go barefooted
and be warm
all the time
not only when you go to bed
and sleep

Moment

Each moment is infinite and complete.

After you get up to go and I can think of no more reasons
for you to stay that I can say without making it all too
  plain,
more plain than what is safe later to look at after we have
  both
had our way with each other and we don't know yet where
  to go
with each other or even if we want to, we stand out in
  front
of the house like proper would-be lovers courting
in an earlier century
I start staring up at the stars because I want to see a falling
  star,
and you follow because you have far more experience at
  stargazing
than I. You are quick and see two, but I see none,
only the after-effect of stars in the vicinity of the falling who
  talk
in coded light after the one goes down, "Yonder he goes;
  yonder she runs."
This is what I know they say, but you say this is not so
I only think it is
and I say it is so and how do you know
and you say maybe so.
Then you tell me about light, how old it is and how new,
  how you first
saw time while you sat close by a river that bent; it was
  then and
it was now is now and it was easier for you to live after
  that
or was it before
you know it now.
I do too. You have always been standing under this sky
  with me.

I have always been here somewhere near you.
When you bend down and I arch up, my breasts ending
like starpoints pushing against you,
we make a bow for a moment. You turn your mouth to my
    cheek and say,
"You are beautiful." Then you kiss me.
I look over my shoulder at all those stars and see you.
"You're beautiful."
Now I say that stars that fall are falling in love.
And what do you say then?

Etheridge Knight
1931 – 1991
Poems from Prison

theridge Knight produced a body of important work even though his career was short and filled with personal pain. Born one of seven children on April 29, 1931 in Corinth, Mississippi, he encountered a number of experiences that tested his will and courage.

Knight enlisted in the Army in 1947, and was wounded during the Korean War. He left the Army in 1957. During his early years, Knight became addicted to drugs and alcohol, which led him to a life of crime to support his additions. In 1960, he was arrested for bank robbery and sentenced to serve time in an Indiana state prison. While there, he took an interest in writing and subsequently met the celebrated poet Gwendolyn Brooks who was at the prison to speak to inmates. Later he was inroduced to publisher Dudley Randall and poet Sonia Sanchez. Randall took an interest in Knight's poetry and published his first book of poems, *Poems from Prison,* in 1968. That same year Knight and Sanchez married.

Poems from Prison was well received. Critics were impressed by the intimate and vivid images of prison life portrayed in the collection. One poem in particular, "The Idea of Ancestry," provides a graphic and powerful litany of feelings that reflected Knight's desire to have a spiritual connection with his family lineage. Shirley Lumpkin, a critic for *Modern American Poetry* wrote that "The Idea of Ancestry" is one of the best poems that has been written about Afro-American conception of family history and human interconnections."

When he was released from prison in 1970, Knight continued to pursue his interest in writing. That year, he edited *Black Voices from Prison,* an anthology by inmates from prisons across the country. Many of his own poems were included. Favorable reviews for the book provided many new opportunities for Knight. He taught at the University of Pittsburg, the University of Hartford and at Lincoln University. He also led Free People's poetry workshops, received a National Endowment for the Arts grant (1972) and a Guggenheim Fellowship (1974).

Despite this success, Knight became addicted to drugs again and he and Sanchez divorced. He continued to write, however. In 1973, Broadside Press published *Press Belly Songs and Other Poems,* which some critics called his most important work. Two other published volumes followed: *Born of a Woman* (1980) and *The Essential Etheridge Knight* (1986), which won an American Book Award. Knight died in 1991 from lung cancer, leaving an undeniable legacy of powerful poetry.

A Poem for Myself

(or Blues for a Mississippi Black Boy)

I was born in Mississippi;
I walked barefooted thru the mud.
Born black in Mississippi,
Walked barefooted thru the mud.
But, when I reached the age of twelve
I left that place for good.
My daddy chopped cotton
And he drank his liquor straight.
Said my daddy chopped cotton
And he drank his liquor straight.
When I left that Sunday morning
He was leaning on the barnyard gate.
Left my mama standing
With the sun shining in her eyes.
Left her standing in the yard
With the sun shining in her eyes.
And I headed North
As straight as the Wild Goose Flies,
I been to Detroit & Chicago
Been to New York city too.
I been to Detroit & Chicago
Been to New York city too.
Said I done strolled all those funky avenues
I'm still the same old black boy with the same old
blues.
Going back to Mississippi
This time to stay for good
Going back to Mississippi
This time to stay for good-
Gonna be free in Mississippi
Or dead in the Mississippi mud.

Etheridge Knight   **25**

To Make a Poem in Prison

It is hard
To make a poem in prison.
The air lends itself not
To the singer.
The seasons creep by unseen
And spark no fresh fires.

Soft words are rare, and drunk drunk
Against the clang of keys;
Wide eyes stare fat zeros
And plea only for pity.

Pity is not for the poet;
Yet poems must be primed.
Here is not even sadness for singing,
Not even a beautiful rage rage,
No birds are winging. The air
Is empty of laughter. And love?
Why, love has flown,
Love has gone to glitten.

Last Poets

1968

Gifted Urban Rappers

The history of the Black Arts Movement would be incomplete without including the Last Poets. This ensemble of gifted urban rappers and musicians played a major role in helping to shape the ideology of this important movement and became its most authentic practitioners. The group also paved the way for the Hip Hop Movement that would emerge a generation later.

The Last Poets were formed on the anniversary of Malcolm X's birthday, May 19, 1968. The name Last Poets was inspired by a poem written by the South African poet Willie Kgositsile who wrote, "When the moment hatches in time's womb there will be no art talk . . . The only person you will hear will be the spear point pivoted in the punctured marrow of the villain . . . Therefore we are the last poets of the world."

The words of Kgositsile motivated the Last Poets to recite poetry that was political and revolutionary. As products of the urban streets of Harlem, New York, the Last Poets were able to translate street vernacular into pulsating rhythms and percussive verbal verse. Although their poetry was offensive to some people, they believed it was necessary to expose the hypocrisy of America and challenge Black people to do something about their condition.

The founding members included David Nelson, Gylan Kain and Abiodun Oyewole. Later Felipe Luciano, Umar Bin Hassan, Jalal Mansur Nuriddin and Suleiman el-Hadi joined. When Oyewole was sentenced to 14 years in prison after being found guilty of robbery, he was replaced by percussionist Nilajah.

The Last Poets produced a number of important albums during the early 1970s. Their initial release, *The Last Poets* (1970), reached the top ten among Billboard's best-selling albums. It was followed by *This Is Madness* (1971) and *Chastisement* (1972).

Because of their affiliation with organizations such as the Student Non-Violent Coordinating Committee (SNCC), the SDS (Students for a Democratic Society) and the Black Panther Party, members of the group were often harrassed by the police and FBI. There were also disagreements among the members and they eventually split into different groups.

Today, many of the rappers of the hip-hop generation have acknowledged the influence and impact of the Last Poets. And after 40 years, The Last Poets (Abiodun Oyewole, Umar Bin Hassan, and percussionist Babatunde) are still writing and performing and have appeared onstage with artists such as Common and Kanye West.

Oh! My People

My people are Black, beige, yellow,
Brown and beautiful.
A garden of life,
with a love as sweet as scuppernong wine,
Growing in muddy waters,
Making brown babies with,
Pink feet and quick minds.

My people warm sometimes hot,
Always cool always together.

My people,
Let's be together.
Understand that we've lived together,
Understand that we've died together,
Understand my brother that I've,
Smelled your piss in my hallway,
And it smell just like mine.
Understand that I love your woman,
My sister,
And her rare beauty,
Is reason enough for a revolution.

Yes, sister, my honest sister,
I have had ugly moments with you,
But you are the only beauty I've ever known.

Yes sister my honest sister,
You are the joy in my smile.
You are the reality of my dreams.
You are the only sister I have,
And I need you.

I need you to feed the children of our race,
I need you to feed the lovers of our race,
I need you to be the summer of my winters,

I need you because,
You are the natural life in the living.
At night there is a moon to make the Blackness be felt.
I am that Blackness,
Filling up the world with My soul,
And the world knows me.
You are that moon,
My moon Goddess shining down light,
On my Black face that fills the universe.
My moon, I am your sun,
And I shall take this peace of light and build a world.

For you my sister,
Sometimes the waters are rough,
And the hungry tide swallows the shore,
Washing away all memories,
Of children's footsteps playing in the sand.

Where is the world I promised my son?
Must he push back the tide
And build the world
That I have rapped about?
Am I so godly until I forget
What a man is?
Am I so right until,
There is no room for patience?

My brother, Oh in brother!
Father of a son,
Father of a warrior.
My brother the sun,
My brother the warrior.
Be the beginning and the end,
For my sister,
Be the revolution for our world.
Turn yourself into yourself,
And then onto this disordered world,
And arrange the laughter for joy,
The tears for sorrow.

Turn purple pants, alligator shoes,
Leather jackets, brown boots,
Polka dot ties, silk suits;
Turn miniskirts, false eyelashes,
Red wigs, afro wigs, Easter bonnets,
Bellbottoms;
Turn this confusion into Unity! Unity!
So that the sun will follow,
Our foot steps in the day.
So that the moon will glow,
In our living rooms at night.
So that food, clothing, and shelter,
Will be free.
Because we are born free,
To have the world as our playground.
My people.

Haki R. Madhubuti
b. 1942
Institution Builder

*H*aki R. Madhubuti is the name most often associated with the Black Arts Movement. Not only did he incorporate the concepts of Black nationalism and Black identity in his writings, he also established institutions where these concepts were put into practice.

Born Don Luther Lee in 1942 in Little Rock, Arkansas, Madhubuti was raised in Detroit with his mother and sister. When he was 16, his mother died from a drug overdose. So the teenager moved to Chicago where he finished high school. After high school, Madhubuti served in the U.S. Army for three years (1960–1963). His experiences there cemented his interest and commitment to the struggle for Black freedom.

Following his release from military service, Madhubuti became an apprentice and curator at the DuSable Museum of African History (1963–1967) in Chicago where he worked closely with Margaret Burroughs, a scholar of pan-African history. The four years he spent at the museum gave him the opportunity to meet some of the world's most prominent Black artists and thinkers. Among them was Gwendolyn Brooks, who encouraged him to publish a collection of his poetry. *Black Pride* was self-published in 1966, and in 1967, it was released by Broadside Press.

This collection introduced a different style of poetry, a style that included the invention of words and a staccato, explosive rhythm whose themes focused on the creation of a Black identity, self-reliance and social protest. In 1968, another collection, *Think Black* followed. Soon, Madhubuti was in demand to speak and read his poetry on college campuses around the country. When his third book, *Don't Cry, Scream!* was published in 1969, Madhubuti's stature as one of America's most celebrated writers was firmly established.

But Madhubuti's success as a writer was only a part of the important contributions he made to the Black Arts Movement. In 1968, using a $400 honorarium he earned from a poetry reading, and with the help of fellow poets Carolyn M. Rodgers and Johari Amini, he started Third World Press. Today, the company is the nation's oldest independent publisher of Black thought and literature. In 1970, Madhubuti, his wife, Dr. Safisha Madhubuti and Soyini Walton, started the Institute of Positive Education to foster a curriculum of Afrocentric education. Today, the Institute operates three African-centered schools in Chicago.

During the early years of the Black Arts Movement, Madhubuti and a number of other Black artists founded the Organization of Black American Culture, a city-wide arts and culture group. And in 1971, along with Larry Neal, he established the *Black Books Bulletin*, a quarterly publication that provided a forum for Black thought for eight years.

Among the books of poetry authored by Madhubuti include *Book of Life* (1973), *Killing Memory, Seeking Ancestors* (1987), *GroundWork: New and Selected Poems from 1966-1996* (1996). He is also the author of *From Plan* to *Planet-Life Studies: The Need for Afrikan Minds and Institutions* (1973), *Enemies: The Clash of Races* (1978) and *Black Men: Obsolete, Single, Dangerous,* two collections of essays.

Today, in addition to serving as publisher of Third World Press and head of the Institute for Positive Education, Madhubuti is director of the Gwendolyn Brooks Center and is a professor of English at Chicago State University. He has received many awards and honors and continues to employ the ideals of the Black Arts Movement in his life and work.

But He Was Cool,
or: he even stopped for green lights

super-cool
ultrablack
a tan/purple
had a beautiful shade.

he had a double-natural
that wd put the sisters to shame.
his dashikis were tailor made
& his beads were imported sea shells
     (from some blk/country i never heard of)
he was triple-hip.

his tikis were hand carved
out of ivory
& came express from the motherland.
he would greet u in swahili
& say good-bye in yoruba.
wooooooooooooo-jim he bes so cool & ill tel li gent

       cool-cool is so cool he was un-cooled by other
         niggers' cool
       cool-cool ultracool was bop-cool/ice box cool so cool
         cold cool
       his wine didn't have to be cooled, him was air
         conditioned cool
       cool-cool/real cool made me cool—now ain't that
         cool
       cool-cool so cool him nick-named refrigerator.

cool-cool so cool
he didn't know,

Haki R. Madhubuti   **35**

after detroit, newark, chicago &c.,
we had to hip
        cool-cool/ super-cool/ real cool
that

to be black
is
to be
very-hot.

change-up

change-up,
let's go for ourselves
both cheeks are broken now.
change-up,
move past the corner bar,
let yr/spirit lift u above that quick high.
change-up,
that tooth pick you're sucking on was
once a log.
change-up,
and yr/children will look at u differently
than   we looked at our parents

blackwoman

will define herself. naturally. will
talk/walk/live/& love her images. her
beauty will be. the only way to be is
to be. blackman take her. u don't need
music to move; yr/movement toward her
is music. & she'll do more than dance.

Larry Neal
1937 – 1981
BAM Philosopher

*L*arry Neal's writings and teachings were influential in defining and describing the role of arts in the African-American struggle for empowerment. As a writer and scholar he helped to shape the ideology of the Black Arts Movement more than any other Black thinker of his time.

Neal felt that Western art traditions weren't always conducive to capturing and reflecting the Black experience.

"New constructs will have to be developed," he wrote. "We will have to alter our concepts of what art is, of what it is supposed to do."

Neal was born in 1937 in Atlanta, Georgia and grew up in Philadelphia. He completed his undergraduate work at Lincoln University and received a Master's degree from the University of Pennsylvania. He was a regular contributor to the *Liberator Magazine, Black Theater Magazine* and *Black World*, formerly *Negro Digest*. Neal taught at Yale, Howard, Wesleyan and at several other institutions and in 1971, he received a prestigious Guggenheim Fellowship for critical studies in Afro-American culture.

In 1965, Neal, along with writer Amiri Baraka and others, founded the Black Arts Repertory Theater and School. Located in Harlem, the theater included classes and workshops in the arts. Its opening is often cited as marking the beginning of the Black Arts Movement. In 1966 and 1967, Neal wrote a number of essays published in *Negro Digest* that explored the relationship between Black music and Black musicians to a Black aesthetic. They would help to place him in the forefront of those defining and establishing the political and cultural foundation for Black arts.

In 1968, Neal and Baraka edited the definitive anthology of the Black Arts Movement, *Black Fire: An Anthology of Afro-American Writing*. It introduced the works of writers such as Sonia Sanchez, Ed Bullins, Lindsey Barrett, Marvin X, Charles Fuller, William Mahoney and Harold Cruse to a wider audience. Alain Locke's *The New Negro* is said to have captured the spirit of the Harlem Renaissance. *Black Fire* did likewise for the Black Arts Movement. Neal wrote two important essays in the anthology that helped to define the new movement. He also co-edited a collection of essays *Trippin, A Need For Change* (1969), with Baraka and A. B. Spellman.

Neal authored two volumes of poetry, *Black Boogaloo: Notes on Black Liberation* (1969) and *Hoodoo Hollerin Bebop Ghosts* (1974). He also wrote a number of plays and many essays and articles. His commitment to creativity and activism provided an early model for the Black Arts Movement. He also brought a keener focus to the relationship among music, drama, literature and folklore. When Larry Neal died in 1981, the Black Arts Movement lost one of its most articulate scholars and visionaries.

For Black Writers
and Artists

How many of them
die their deaths
between the slow rhythms and the quick,
between going and becoming.
time does not kill, life does, in
swift moments of hate. careless steps.
sharp glances over your shoulder.

So many of them . . . across dark oceans,
in smelly cafes, or along foreign banks,
or in the countess's penthouse,
or on the avenues of speechlessness
where they have been made to
prostitute their blood
to the Merchants of War that manifestly loom
behind large heads and large glasses,
who explode no myths and who are themselves
makers of myth.

How many of them die their deaths
looking for the sun, finding darkness in the city of lights.
motherless. whirling in a world of empty words,
snatching at, and shaping the rubbish
that is our lives,
until form becomes, or life dances to an incoherent finish.

Larry Neal   **39**

Holy Days

HOLY THE DAYS OF THE OLD PRUNE FACE
  JUNKIE MEN.
HOLY THE SCAG FILLED ARMS.
HOLY THE HARLEM FACES
LOOKING FOR SPACE IN THE DEAD ROCK VALLEYS
  OF THE CITY

HOLY THE FLOWERS
SING HOLY FOR THE RAPED HOLIDAYS
AND BESSIES GUTS SPILLING ON THE MISSISSIPPI
  ROAD
SING HOLY FOR ALL OF THE FACES THAT INCHED
TOWARD FREEDOM, FOLLOWED THE NORTH STAR
  LIKE
HARRIET AND DOUGLASS.
SING HOLY FOR ALL OUR SINGERS AND SINNERS
AND ALL OF THE SHAPES AND STYLES AND FORMS
OF OUR LIBERATION,
HOLY, HOLY, HOLY, FOR THE MIDNIGHT HASSLES
FOR THE GODS OF OUR ANCESTORS BELLOWING
SUNSETS
AND BLUES CHANTING THE TRUTH THAT GAVE US
  VISION
O GOD MAKE US STRONG AND READY
HOLY, HOLY, HOLY FOR THE DAY WE OPEN OUR EYES,
  DIG OURSELVES
AND RAISE IN THE SUN OF OUR OWN PEACE AND
  PLACE AND
SPACE: YES LORD.

Sterling Plumpp
b. 1940
Blues Poet

Sterling D. Plumpp is known for his ability to translate various musical genres, especially blues, into rhythmic patterns of Black dialogue that capture the essence of the Black experience.

Born in Clinton, Mississippi in 1940, he was raised by his sharecropper grandparents, Victor and Mattie Emmanuel. As a young boy, he worked the fields with his parents and did not attend school until he was eight years old. Nonetheless, he graduated from Holy Ghost High School in 1960 and was awarded a scholarship to Saint Benedict College in Atchison, Kansas. There he was introduced to Greek literature, and the work of James Baldwin and Richard Wright, whose writings motivated him to become a writer.

After two years, Plumpp moved to Chicago and worked at the post office before serving in the U.S. Army in 1964 and 1965. After his discharge, he enrolled in Chicago's Roosevelt University, where he earned his B.S. and M.A. degrees in Psychology.

Plumpp's involvement in the Black Arts Movement began when he joined the Writer's Workshop of the Organization of Black American Culture (OBAC). Under the guidance of Hoyt W. Fuller, editor of *Black World* (formerly *Negro Digest*), the workshop, which also attracted Don L. Lee (Haki R. Madhubuti), Carolyn M. Rodgers, Johari Amini and Sam Greenlee, author of *The Spook Who Sat By The Door*, helped aspiring writers develop their craft. Plumpp's first collection of poetry, *Portable Soul* (1969), was published by Third World Press. *Half Black, Half Blacker* (1970), *Black Rituals* (1974), and *Steps to Break the Circle (1974)* helped to establish Plumpp as an important writer. *Muslim Men* (1972) and *Clinton* (1976) were also added to the canon.

South African poet Keorapetse Kgositsile praised him as a writer with a "level of social consciousness." But Plumpp's "social consciousness" is not confined to Black America. It also includes the Black Diaspora and Africa. Two significant works in this area include *Somehow We Survive: An Anthology of South African Writing* (1981), which he edited, and *Johannesburg and Other Poems* (1993).

In 2003, the publication of *Velvet BeBop Kente Cloth* enhanced Mr. Plumpp's literary legacy and was acknowledged by Reginald Gibbons, Professor of English, Northwestern University as ". . . amazing utterances filled with metaphor and originality of expression." After 25 years of teaching at the University of Illinois at Chicago, Plumpp retired and was named Professor Emeritus.

Sterling Plumpp continues to write and teach part-time in the Master of Fine Arts Program at Chicago State University.

Poem

(for the Blues Singers)

Poems are not places.
There are no maps for centuries
where the geography of skin
is anonymous in memory.
I am a secondhand dream
in concrete slabs of silence.
Somewhere bones speak
for my name/ over fibers
of their secrets. My poems
are wanderers, meandering
in crevices between distances
and tombs. Where my voice
is bound with hammering against
the anvil of truth.

Poems are bridges, neon
reaches across worlds
where language seeks
a voice for itself. Where words
are steps up towers
of perception. I exist
in language I invent
out of ruins. Out of
the nameless sand wind
scatters as my soul.
I exist in lines of spirits.
Who gather in longings
blues singers peddle for
sweat. I exist, landless,
cropping my dreams in soil
from distances and silence
only travelers of the Middle Passage
own.

Sterling Plumpp

Ten.

Dizzy say/All
the time/Government
Wanna know/How to
do nothing/Why they
arrest so/Many cats.
Stop them/Harass them
or/Jail them. Say/Cats
say they/*Ain't* done
nothng or/*Ain't* got
nothing/He say Bird
the/First cat to do
or/Riff nothing. He/Say
if you tell/Law you *done*
nothing/Or you *got*
nothing/Say you gone
to some/Laboratory fore
you kin/Blink your eye.
Say/They gotta cut
or/Crush every tissue.
Looking/For clues
to/Nothing. Say/So
much/Nothing exist and
They/Don't own an ounce.

Bird is/A poet. A lyric/Self
discovery and/Birth. He
grimace every/Time
he blow/Line
ages of/Fragmentary diaries
of wind/He
find in/Cell
blocks of space/He birth
home/Screaming to know
landscapes/Of his horn.
Fred/Can
do more in a/Second

hand riff/Than composers
reveal in/Three dozen
scores/They write
because they can/Neither reed
or/Rite.

I hear/Him say:
like Bird/I play
in/Tongues of spirits
that ain't/Born and
ain't/Never been dead.
I play/Be-Bop Fred.

Sterling Plumpp

Eugene Redmond

1937

Renaissance Griot

Some have called Eugene B. Redmond the "Renaissance Griot" of the Black Arts Movement. A multi-faceted artist and scholar, Redmond's writings span a number of literary genres. Like many other writers of the Black Arts Movement, he was committed to raising the consciousness of Black people to achieve empowerment and cultural independence. An activist and writer, he played a major role in helping to shape the ideology of the Black Arts Movement.

Born in 1937, Redmond is a native of East St. Louis, Illinois, where he has been its Poet Laureate since 1976. He began writing for his high school newspaper. From 1958 to 1961, Redmond served as a U.S. Marine in the Far East. Upon his return to the States, he worked as an associate editor of the *East St. Louis Beacon*. Two years later, he co-founded a weekly paper in East St. Louis, the *Monitor*, working at different times as a contributing editor, executive editor, and editor of the editorial page. He earned a B.A. in English Literature from Southern Illinois University (1964) and a M.A. in English Literature from Washington University (1966).

In 1965, while still in graduate school, Redmond won first prize in the Washington University Annual Festival of the Arts for his poem *"The Eye in the Ceiling."* In 1968 he published his first volume of poetry, *A Tale of Two Toms, or Tom-Tom.* Subsequent volumes include *A Tale of Time & Toilet Tissue* (1969), *Sentry of the Four Golden Pillars* (1970), *River of Bones and Flesh and Blood* (1971), *Songs from an Afro/Phone* (1972), *Consider Loneliness as These Things* (1973), *In a Time of Rain & Desire* (1973), and *The Eye in the Ceiling* (1991). *The Eye in the Ceiling* won a American Book Award. Three of these collections were published by the Black Writers Press, which Redmond founded with fellow poet and friends Henry Dumas and Sherman Fowler. Redmond has been poet-in-residence at Oberlin College, California State University, the University of Wisconsin and Wayne State University.

Redmond has edited a number of books and journals on Black writing, including *Drumvoices: The Mission of Afro-American Poetry, A Critical History* (1976). This survey of poetry from 1746 to 1976, which took eight years to research, explores the beliefs, customs, traditions and practices that tie Black cultures to their African origins. Redmond is also Henry Dumas' literary executor and has edited seven volumes of Dumas' work, including *Goodbye Sweet-water* (1988) and *Knees of a Natural Man* (1989). Redmond has also worked diligently to preserve the legacy of Katherine Dunham, the late African-American dancer and cultural icon.

Redmond's poetic style displays his knowledge of the spoken word and performance. He sees basic rhythms and music as keys to a distinct style of African American writing. Many of his poems have a rap-like beat and contain direct references to jazz, blues, spirituals, soul music, and black musicians. A professor at Southern Illinois University since 1990, Redmond continues to write and pass on the legacy of Black literature to a new generation.

Eugene Redmond

The Eye in the Ceiling

You sit snug in my ceiling
Staring at the room
While insects worship you.

But I can hide you in the night
And you body like a corpse
Loses its heat in seconds.

This time however
Resurrection is simple,
Far simpler than the painful
Mathematics of your birth:

Though in your final death
I'll go through the clumsy
Ritual of winding you,

Knowing I could not
Have touched you
in your citadel an hour ago.

Consider Loneliness as These Things

Consider loneliness a lull,
As some secret space that jails in the mind,
As a circumstantial melody: the blues of
Wretchedness or the blues of joy;
As some totem of penitence or pity or pride,
Sagging from the neck like a lead medallion
Or a dead bird:
Spinning out,
Spinning out wire-threads or hardfeathers of
    confinement;
As a hypnotist, eye-blind, with psychic sight
And strength to unleash the lances of unexpurgated pain,
Of unquelled thought-quakes, or Watusi-tall dreams.
Consider loneliness as these things.

Consider loneliness as a weaver of want,
As a giver of needs undefined,
As some ancestral repository
For a personal mythic tablet;
As a nerve, nudged overgently —
Or laced with worry;
As a womb, wailing out its
Liquid waifs, its tight lips waiting,
Waiting . . .
As a tyrant, timeless and elastic —
Consider loneliness.

Eugene Redmond

Carolyn M. Rodgers

b. 1945

Powerful Female Voice

uring the Black Arts Movement, the writing of Carolyn M. Rodgers was a standard for articulating poetry's role as a creative force to liberate Black people from oppression. Rodgers' early work was thematically militant in tone and stubbornly independent of standardized verses and traditional poetic styles and forms. Her distinctive voice and feminist perspective often drew criticism from some of her contemporaries.

Born in Chicago in 1945, Rodgers earned a Bachelor of Arts degree from Roosevelt University in 1965 and a Master of Arts degree from the University of Chicago in 1980. A social worker by profession, Rodgers was employed with the Young Men's Christian Association (YMCA) from 1963 to 1968 before embarking on her literary career.

A founding member of Chicago's Organization of Black American Culture Writer's Workshop, she was often at odds with some of her male counterparts regarding the role of Black women in the movement. In December 1967, along with Haki R. Madhubuti, and Johari Amini, Rodgers helped found Third World Press, an outlet for African-American literature. Third World Press published her first three books *Paper Soul* (1968), *Songs of A Blackbird* (1969) and *2 Love Rags* (1969). Later, she moved to Broadside Press of Detroit, founded by poet and critic Dudley Randall. Her next four collections were published by Broadside.

In the mid-seventies, Rodgers' poetry began to change thematically, reflecting a more introspective and spiritual vision of life. She moved to Doubleday/Anchor, which published *how I got ovah: New and Selected Poems* (1975). This outstanding volume of poetry demonstrated Rodgers' ability to use traditional poetic forms without sacrificing her passion for Black dialogue. Hilda Njoki McElroy, a noted critic, said the volume "reveals Rodgers' transformation from a militant Black woman to a woman intensely concerned with God, traditional values, and her private self."

Rodgers has taught and lectured at many colleges, including Indiana University, Roosevelt University, Fisk University, Emory University and Harold Washington College. She received a National Endowment for the Arts grant (1970) and the Poet Laureate Award of the Society of Midland Authors and a Carnegie Award (1979).

In her analysis of Rodgers' work, Jean Davis, a critic for the *Dictionary of Literary Biography,* said she was "one of the most sensitive and complex poets to emerge from this movement and struggle with its contradictions."

Not About Poems

a lonely poem is nothing
special

  like a lonely person
   you can see them everyday
nobody wants to read a
  lonely poem
like nobody wants to read a
  lonely face
   you see them every day

i can write about love
living high and fine togethers

i can write about mommas, poppas,
show-stoppers & blues
i can write about dreams and
schemes, living & dying
getting down, losing & grooving
i can write about almost anything—

  but a lonely poem ain't got
no audience
  cause it bleeds all over the page
hits and haunts your face
  hurts your heart as much as your eyes (can you hurt)
a lonely poem ain't about poems
  cause it hurts your heart as much as your eyes
   i say
oh say
can you hurt

who needs me . . .

how i got ovah II/ It Is Deep II

(for Evangelist Richard D. Henton)

just when i thought i had gotten away my mother
called me on the phone
and did not ask,
but commanded me
to come to church with her.

and because i knew so much
and had "escaped"
i thought it a harmless enough act.

i was not prepared for the Holy Ghost.
i was not prepared to be covered by the
blood of Jesus.

i was not ready to be dipped in
the water. . . .
i could not drink the water turned wine.

and so i went back another day
trying to understand the mysteries
of mystical life the "intellectual"
purity of mystical light.
and that Sunday evening while i was
sitting there and the holy gospel choir
was singing
"oh oh oh oh somebody touched me"
somebody touched me.
and when i turned around to
see what, it was whoever touched me wanted
my mother leaned over and whispered in my ear
        "musta been the hand of the Lord"

Carolyn M. Rodgers

Kalamu Ya Salaam
b. 1947
BAM South

*K*alamu Ya Salaam's contributions to the Black Arts Movement are enormous. A great communicator, Salaam has used his talents as a writer, educator, playwright, essayist and activist to educate Black people about the importance of culture and art to Black Liberation.

Salaam played a major role in bringing the Black Arts Movement to the South. Salaam, whose birth name is Vallery Ferdinand III, was born in 1947 in New Orleans, Louisiana's Ninth Ward. After attending Carlton College in Northfield, Minnesota for two years (1964–1965) he served three years in the U.S. Army. When he returned to New Orleans, he attended Delgado Junior College where he received an Associate degree. It was during this period that he became associated with the Free Southern Theater.

During the 1960s this pioneering group brought theatrical productions to the South. Several of Salaam's plays, including "The Picket" (1968), "Black Liberation Army" (1969), and "Happy Birthday Jesus" (1969), were produced by the group. Salaam and Tom Dent went on to found BLKARTSOUTH, which evolved out of a Free Southern Theater writers' workshop first organized by Dent. BLKARTSOUTH helped to develop young writers in the New Orleans area and published *NKOMBO*, a quarterly journal of poetry, prose, fiction and drama.

Salaam's first book of poetry, *The Blues Merchant*, was published in 1969. Other volumes published during the Black Arts Movement include *Hofu Ni Kwenu* (1973), *Pamoja Tutashinda* (1974) and *Revolutionary Love* (1978). In 1970, Salaam became editor of *The Black Collegian*, a career and self-development magazine targeted to African-American students and other students of color. In 1973, he helped to found Ahidiana, a Pan-African Nationalist organization that served preschool children and he directed Essence of Life, a poetry and music ensemble that gained international status. Salaam also founded Runagate Press, NOMMO Literary Society and currently maintains an informational listserv that serves Black writers and others worldwide.

Salaam has received many honors and recognitions for his work, including a Senior Literature Fellowship (1999), Endowment for the Humanities Award (1998), and the Mayor Marc Mortal Arts Award (New Orleans, 1997).

Salaam is one of the most prolific writers and creators of African American discourse in the late twentieth century. Still residing in New Orleans, he continues to add to his enormous body of artistic and cultural work.

Lament

/for black men everywhere/

when
  will our men be men
       not of fear and trembling
       feeding dark soil with their own
  dark blood or
       crying yes sirs and halting steps
  of broken airs about
  themselves
but men:
  simply able to love their lives
  as men are said to do?
God can you possibly
replenish that lost seed
  who were once lovely African chieftains,
       princes and such, loving
       their queens
  Can pride be restored
  or must they suffer forever
  attempting a shield of their
  impotence from our knowing eyes.

INSPIRATION
THE FLOWER IN THE HOUSE, THE AIR
WE BLACK MEN BREATHE

love a good woman
love a good woman
for all the time there is
for all the life there is
for all the best we are
love a good woman
love a woman
love love a good woman
in sunshine, in rain, place
yr house in order, in
balanced on the tear drop of her happiness
on the hair back from her geled* head
on the soft steps she makes
moving toward you being the flower in the house
yr oxygen, yr gettin up fuel
yr no nonsense and strength to do what you got to do
the love of a good woman
loving you love a good woman
yr choice, companion and soul mate,
yr maker really, if you be man
then woman is yr maker, yr woman is yr maker
yr black woman is yr creator, woman
is what you should love yr good woman
is what you need yr good woman to love, to live
yr pleasant voice in the evening and smiles in yr morning
yr soft fingers touch on yr chest calling you king
calling you man, calling you god
you god the giver come on now love yr good woman
she creator the maker, love yr good woman
no man makes himself
woman makes man and love
love a good woman
sister i am incomplete
without you, i am vessel full

Kalamu Ya Salaam   **57**

of holes, i am spirit begging
substance, i am shadow with
our form, i am baby wait
ing to be born, i am that faggot
walking down the street
not knowing what to do with myself
like singers without song
i need yr tender touch

*head wrapped respectfully Afrikan styled

Sonia Sanchez
b. 1934
Cultural Icon

Sonia Sanchez's name has become synonymous with audacity, spirituality and artistic innovation. These qualities have helped to make her a cultural icon in the Black community.

Born Wilsonia Benita Driver in Birmingham, Alabama, Sanchez emerged as one of the most significant writers of the Black Arts Movement. As are many other Black poets of the 1960s, Sanchez is a multifaceted writer, but poetry remains her most passionate form of literary expression. She is best noted for her uncanny ability to translate certain phonics in the English language into abbreviated phrases that speak directly to people. One of her strongest admirers, poet Kalamu Ya Salaam, stated that "in her work from the 1960s, Sanchez restructured traditional English grammar to suit her interest in Black speech pattern." Fellow writer Haki R. Madhubiti said that Sanchez, "more than any other poet he has been responsible for legitimizing the use of urban Black English in written form."

Sanchez graduated from Hunter College of the City University of New York in 1955 and did postgraduate study at New York University. Her training at these schools helped her to develop as a serious scholar of literature.

During the 1950s and 1960s, she was involved in the Civil Rights Movement. Her first published book of poetry, *Homecoming,* was released in 1969. It was followed by *We a BaddDDD People* (1970) and *Liberation Poems* (1971). Other collections followed, establishing Sanchez as a major literary figure. She recorded albums and authored a number of plays, including "The Bronx Is Next" (1968) and "Sister Sonji" (1970). In 1995 she won an American Book Award for the poetry compilation, *Homegirls and Handgrenades.*

Sanchez's poetry is rooted in the rhythms of Black street vernacular and focuses on heightening the consciousness of African Americans who hide their Blackness because of self-denial, self-contempt and mis-education. She has also mastered the technique of writing haiku, brief three-line verses that can capture the essence of a person's feelings or convey a visual picture of magnitude. Sanchez's writings are included in all the important Black literary anthologies. She has lectured at more than 300 colleges in America and taught at institutions such as Amherst College, Rutgers University, Spelman College and Temple University. She has been the recipient of many prestigious honors and awards, including the PEN Writing Award (1969), National Endowment for the Arts (1978), American Book Award (1985), National Institute of Arts and Letters Grant (1970) and she received an honorary doctorate from Wilberforce University in 1972.

Some of the Black poets who supported the Black Arts Movement in the 1960s and 1970s no longer embrace its ideology. Sanchez, however, has never wavered from its original purpose. She continues to raise the consciousness of people through her writing and activism. Many younger poets and rappers in turn embrace her work. Sanchez is also a supporter of their right to express themselves in new ways, perhaps remembering what she faced when she was one the creators of a "new kind of writing" that helped to define the Black Arts Movement.

Father and Daughter

1.

it is difficult to believe that we
ever talked. how did we spend the night
while seasons passed in place of words? Outright
nothing is ever lost; save fantasy
that painted plastic walls with shades and
rolled soft violets while red fruit fell.
along your distant shore i heard you tell
of swollen dawns, and as you crossed the land
of stones you did not turn to sift the
mirror of my sands. This is your caress
in me the wings of owls who gathered flesh
began to turn and gave affinity to skillful breaths that
    filled the air
with screaming. Who screams? life is everywhere.

2.

you cannot live here and bend my heart
amid the rhythms of your screams. Apart
still venom sleeps and drains down through the years
touch not these hands once live with shears
i live a dream about you; each man
alone. You need the sterile woods old age can
bring, no opening of the veins whose smell
might bruise light breasts and burst our shell
of seeds. the landslide of your season
bums the air: this mating has no reason.
don't cry, late grief is not enough. the motion
of your tides still flows within: the ocean
of deep blood that drowns the land we die:
while young moons rage and wander in the sky.

Sonia Sanchez   **61**

Last Poem I'm Gonna Write Bout Us

some
   times i dream bout
         u&me
           runnen down
a street laughen.
      me no older
      u no younger
         than we be.
& we finalee catch
      each other.
         laugh.   tooouch
in the nite.
    some
      times
        i turn a comer
of my mind
    & u be there
        looooooking
          at me.
& smilen.
   yo/far/away/smile.
       & i moooove
to u.
  & the day is not any day. & yes ter day
is looonNNg
    goooNNe. & we just be. Some
times i be steady dreamen bout u
        cuz i waaannNt
neeeeEEecD u so
    baaaaAdDD.
  with u no younger &
  me no older
    than we be.

This Is Not a Small Voice

This is not a small voice
you hear   this is a large
voice coming out of these cities.
This is the voice of LaTanya.
Kadesha. Shaniqua. This
is the voice of Antoine.
Darryl. Shaquille.
Running over waters
navigating the hallways
of our schools spilling out
on the corners of our cities and
no epitaphs spill out of their river mouths.

This is not a small love
you hear   this is a large
love, a passion for kissing learning
on its face.
This is a love that crowns the feet with hands
that nourishes, conceives, feels the water sails
mends the children,
folds them inside our history where they
toast more than the flesh
where they suck the bones of the alphabet
and spit out closed vowels.
This is a love colored with iron and lace.
This is a love initialed Black Genius.

This is not a small voice
you hear.

Sonia Sanchez

63

Askia Muhammad Touré
b. 1938
BAM Architect

Askia Muhammad Touré was one of the earliest and most forceful voices in the Black Arts Movement. He helped to define the movement's purpose and goals and helped to introduce it to many parts of the country. His important contributions, however, have largely gone unappreciated.

Touré was a founding member of Umbra Writers' Workshop, a group that helped to set the stage for the Black Arts Movement. Organized in New York City in 1962, Umbra comprised writers, artists and activists who sought to integrate the arts with a distinct Black identity and focus. Other members included David Henderson, Ishmael Reed, Joe Johnson, Norman Pritchard, Calvin Hernton, Tom Dent and Archie Shepp. The group published *Umbra* magazine from 1962 to 1963 and Touré served as the publication's art director. Umbra disbanded in 1964, but Touré remained active and continued to advocate for art that reflected the Black struggle and Black aspirations. From 1963 to 1965, he served on the editorial board of *Black America,* the literary arm of the Black Nationalist Revolutionary Action Movement. The following two years he was on the staff of *Liberator Magazine,* and then served as an associate editor of *Black Dialogue,* and editor-in-chief of the *Journal of Black Poetry,* which grew out of *Black Dialogue.* These publications offered important forums for Black writers. They also provided Touré with the opportunity to play a role in helping establish a foundation for the Black Arts Movement. In 1965, he helped author the Student National Coordinating Committee's Black Power position paper that, among other things, called for the creation of Black-led political groups across the United States. Larry Neal, a leader of the Black Arts Movement, would later write, "Black Art is the aesthetic and spiritual sister of the Black Power concept. As such, it envisions an art that speaks directly to the needs and aspirations of Black America."

Born Rolland Snellings in Raleigh, North Carolina in 1938, Touré moved with his father, mother, and younger brother to Dayton, Ohio when he was six years old. After graduating from high school, he joined the Air Force, serving from 1956 to 1959. In 1960, he moved to New York to study painting at the Arts Students League.

During the mid 1960s, Touré moved to California where he taught African history in the first Africana Studies program located at a majority university, San Francisco State College.

Touré's published works include *Juju: Magic Songs for the Black Nation* (1970), *Songhai!* (1972) and *From the Pyramids to the Projects* (1990), which was an American Book Award winner.

Touré, who lives in Atlanta, still writes and has taught at Clark-Atlanta University, continuing the tradition of the Black Arts Movement. Since 1988, he has played a major role in shaping and organizing the city's National Black Arts Festival. He has also spearheaded a campaign to introduce Africana Studies in Atlanta Public Schools.

A Song for Patriots 2 / Rhythm & Blues

So what to this earth do we bring
As definers and defenders of Soul?
How do we imagine, or shape, Reality to our
Collective complexities, we innovative
Creators of "Jazz"? We sable knights
Of auction blocks, we inhibitors of projects,
Keepers of spicy gumbo, aristocrats
Of appetite evolved to aromatic barbeque;
Queens of bimsha-rhythmic erotica, sultans
Of slam-dunking Summer with its romance
And reggae magic, among festivals
Blessed with myriad Nubian profiles.
Who gives voice to Vision/Memory within
This Nation of wounded geniuses, wild with
Bluesy love songs, ominous with gangsta-rap,
Moaning at the graves of murdered prophets?
A people who refuse to "break a sweat"
In the wake of "crack," "heroin," "ice," HIV,
Killer cops and other barbaric acts.
A people who spitefully spit in the eyes of Death
On a daily basis—and make him blink.
A people with a curious love for grape soda,
Cadillacs, and other people's gods.
A people who turn gray Puritan Sundays into an
Elegant, tropical Fashion Show—with coiffures
Of feathered flare and sensual sassiness.
A people who transformed basketball into a Cosmic
Ballet of Watusi demigods, challenging flight.
A people who demand Freedom's uncompromising
Light in a profit-driven nightmare of game show
Robots and Media whores.
A people this poet loves with a furious passion!

Survival: A Chant
(for Martin, Malcolm and Medgar)

Paint this joy upon the World's canvas;
that despite lynchings, bombings,
dirty deeds, we living seeds of a Bantu
Nation live and breathe amidst the trials
and madness of Anglo-sponsored
profiteers, spawn of puritans, new breed
pioneers raping this world with Saxon greed.
We are Thirty Million strong, bred from auction
blocks of chained chattels. Slaves!—bought and
sold like tamed cattle—now produce astronauts,
rocket scientists, while sermons from
slain kings rattle in America's frigid ears.

Askia Muhammad Touré

Quincy Troupe
b. 1939
A Writer for All Seasons

uincy Troupe emerged from the Black Arts Movement as a major writer whose works have received national and international acclaim. Born in New York City in 1939, Troupe moved to East St. Louis, Illinois where his early writing career began. There he met and became friends with fellow writers Eugene Redmond and Henry Dumas. Troupe's father was a catcher in the Negro Baseball League. In 1945 and 1947, he managed the Cleveland Buckeyes to Negro American League titles. Troupe shared that athletic talent and received a baseball scholarship to Grambling State University where he stayed for two years, before joining the U.S. Army. After his discharge, he taught creative writing at the Watts Writers Workshop from 1966 to 1968 and he served as director of the Malcom X Center in Los Angeles during the summers of 1969 and 1970.

In 1964, Troupe's first published poem, "What Is A Black Man" was featured in *Paris Match*, a publication with an international readership. His first collection of poems, *Embryo Poems,* was published in 1972, and included pieces he had written from 1967 to 1971. These poems revealed his keen sense of imagery and mastery of lyrical phrasing. Other published works include *Transcircularities: New and Selected Poems* (2002), *Choruses: Poems* (1999), *Avalanche: Poems* (1996), *Weather Reports: New and Selected Poems* (1991), *Skulls along the River* (1984), and *Snake-Back Solos: Selected Poems 1969–1977* (1979), which received an American Book Award.

Troupe's writings focus on themes related to Black culture and the Third Word. He is a founding editor of *Confrontation: A Journal of Third World Literature* and *American Rag* and has taught Third Word Literature at Columbia University and Ohio University.

In addition to his poetry, Troupe edited the highly acclaimed *James Baldwin: The Legacy* and co-wrote, with the legendary Miles Davis, *Miles, the Autobiography,* which won the American Book Award in 1989.

Troupe became a professor of literature at the University of California, San Diego (UCSD) in 1990 and in 2002, he was selected as the first Poet Laureate of California. However, due to a discrepancy in his official resume, he was forced to resign as laureate and eventually retired from UCSD.

Troupe, whose early writings helped to define the Black Arts Movement, continues to be a major literary figure. In 2006, he collaborated with self-made millionaire Chris Gardner on Gardner's autobiography, *The Pursuit of Happyness.* The book served as the inspiration for a film of the same name that starred Will Smith. Troupe has also written books for children.

Quincy Troupe continues to write, speak and read his work to people around the country and world.

Poem For My Father

for Quincy Troupe, Sr.

father, it was an honor to be there, in the dugout
with you, the glory of great black men swinging their lives
as bats, at tiny white balls
burning in at unbelievable speeds, riding up & in & out
a curve breaking down wicked, like a ball falling off a table
moving away, snaking down, screwing its stitched magic
into chitlin circuit air, its comma seams spinning
again toward breakdown, dipping like a hipster
bebopping a knee-dip stride in the charlie parker forties
wrist curling like a swan's neck
behind a "slick" black back
cupping an invisible ball of dreams

& you there, father, regal as an african obeah man
sculpted out of wood from a sacred tree of no name no place
    origin
thick branches branching down into cherokee & someplace else
    lost
way back in africa, the sap running dry
crossing from north carolina into georgia, inside grandmother
    mary's
womb, where your mother had you in the violence of that red soil
ink blotter news gone now into blood graves
of american blues, sponging rococo
truth long gone as dinosaurs
the agent-oranged landscape of former names
absent of african polysyllables, dry husk consonants there
now in their place, names flat as polluted rivers
& that guitar string smile always snaking across
virulent american redneck faces
scorching, like atomic heat mushrooming over nagasaki
& hiroshima, the fever blistered shadows of it all
inked as etchings into sizzling concrete

but you there father through it all, a yardbird solo
riffin on bat & ball glory, breaking down the fabricated myths
of white major league legends, of who was better than who
beating them at their own crap
game with killer bats, as bud powell swung his silence into beauty
of a josh gibson home run skittering across piano keys of bleachers
shattering all manufactured legends up there in lights
struck out white knights on the risky edge of amazement
awe, the miraculous truth sluicing through
steeped & disguised in the blues
confluencing, like the point at the cross
when a fastball hides itself in a curve breaking
down & away in a wicked sly grin posed as an ass
scratching uncle tom, who like satchel paige
delivering his famed hesitation pitch before coming
back with a hard high fast one, is slicker, sliding
quicker than a professional hit man-
the deadliness of it all, the sudden strike
like that of the "brown bomber's" crossing right
of sugar ray robinson's lightning, cobra bite

& you there father through it all catching rhythms
of chono pozo balls drumming like conga beats into your catcher's
    mitt
hard & fast as "cool papa" bell jumping into bed
before the lights went out

of the old negro baseball league, a promise
a harbinger, of shock waves, soon come

Snow & Ice

ice sheets sweep this slick mirrored dark place
space as keys that turn in tight, trigger
pain of situations
where we move ever so slowly
so gently into time-traced agony
the bright turning of imagination
so slowly
grooved through revolving doors, opening up to enter
mountains where spirits walk voices, ever so slowly
swept by cold, breathing fire
as these elliptical moments of illusion
link fragile loves sunk deep in snows as footprints
the voice prints cold black gesticulations
bone bare voices
chewed skeletal choices
in fangs of piranha gales
spewing out slivers of raucous laughter
glinting bright as hard polished silver nails

OTHER IMPORTANT FIGURES
OF THE BLACK ARTS MOVEMENT

Thomas Covington Dent (1932–1998) was a poet, essayist, oral historian, dramatist, cultural activist and an influential figure during the Black Arts Movement. He was one of the founders of the New York–based Umbra Writer's Workshop, one of the first organizations of Black writers to emerge during the 1960s. In 1965, Dent moved to his native city New Orleans and joined the Free Southern Theater, an activist community theater company. After becoming associate director and helping to organize performances throughout the South, he established the FST Writing Workshop. The workshop later became BLKARTSOUTH, an organization that helped promote the arts throughout the South. Tom Dent published two books of poetry, *Magnolia Street* (1976) *Blue Lights and River Songs* (1982), and in 1969 he co-founded *Callaloo, A Quarterly Black Journal of African American Arts and Letters*. He will be best remembered for helping to bring the Black Arts Movement to the South.

In April 1968, at the age of 33, **Henry Dumas** was shot and killed by a New York Transit Authority Policeman at 125th Street Station in a case of "mistaken identity." At the time of his death, he had finished several manuscripts of poetry and short stories. Following his death, his poetry, short fiction, and novels were published due to the efforts of his friends Eugene Redmond, Toni Morrison, and Quincy

Troupe. *Poetry for My People* was released in 1970 and was published again in 1974 as *Play Ebony, Play Ivory*. In a review of the book, writer Julius Lester called Dumas "the most original Afro-American poet of the sixties." Other published titles include *Arks of Bones and Other Stories* (1974), *Rope of the Wind and Other Stories* (1979), *Knees of a Natural Man: The Selected Poetry of Henry Dumas (1989)*, and the unfinished novel *Jonah and the Green Stone (1976)*. Although his writing career was cut short, Henry Dumas has had a lasting impact on Black literature.

Hoyt Fuller, editor, critic and mentor, was a pivotal figure of the Black Arts Movement. Born in Atlanta and raised in Detroit, he graduated from Wayne State University and began a career in journalism and editing, holding positions with the *Michigan Chronicle*, the *Detroit Tribune*, *Collier's Encyclopedia*, and *Ebony* magazine among other publications. In 1961, after traveling abroad for several years, Fuller was hired to edit *Negro Digest*. Under his leadership, the monthly publication became the leading forum of the emerging Black Arts Movement. In 1970, the publication's name was changed to *Black World* to more accurately reflect its scope, which included Africa and the African diaspora. Fuller was also a founder of Organization of Black American Culture (OBAC), where writers such as Haki Madhubuti, Carolyn M. Rodgers, Nikki Giovanni and Angela Jackson were participants. Hoyt Fuller's impact during the Black Arts Movement was strong and incisive. He influenced the careers of many Black writers and artists.

In his roles as poet and publisher, **Dudley Randall** was the leading exponent of the new Black poetry that emerged during the Black Arts Movement. He founded Broadside Press out of his home in 1965 and ran it nearly single-handedly for a dozen years. The press provided an outlet for Black poets who found it very difficult to get their works published by larger corporate presses. Among the many poets whose works Broadside Press published included Haki Madhubuti, Sonia Sanchez, Etheridge Knight, Audre Lorde, as well as Gwendolyn Brooks, Margaret Walker and James Emanuel. Randall also edited and published anthologies that promoted the works of these writers. A poet himself, his published body of work includes *Poem Counterpoem*, with Margaret Danner (1966), *Cities Burning* (1968) and *More to Remember: Poems of Four Decades* (1971). But it was as a publisher and mentor that Dudley Randall made his most important contributions to the Black Arts Movement.

Marvin X was born Marvin Ellis Jackmon in Fowler, California. During the 1960s he became involved in Black theater, founded his own press, and wrote several plays and volumes of poetry. He is best known, however, for his work as a playwright. Along with Ed Bullins, he founded the Black Arts/West Theatre in San Francisco in 1966. A number of Marvin X's plays were staged in California and around the country during the period. In 1967, Marvin X founded the El Kitab Sudan Publishing Company, which published several of his books of poetry. He remains active as a writer, lecturer and teacher.

SELECTED BIBLIOGRAPHY

Baraka, Amiri, *Blues People: Negro Music in White America*, Greenwood Press, Westport, CT, 1980

Baraka, Amiri, *Dutchman and the Slave: Two Plays*, Faber and Faber, London, UK, 1965

Baraka, Amiri, *It's Nation Time*, Third World Press, Chicago, Illinois, 1970

Evans, Mari, *I Am a Black Woman*, Morrow, New York, NY, 1970

Evans, Mari, *Singing Black: Alternative Nursery Rhymes for Children*, Just Us Books, Incorporated, East Orange, NJ 1998

Evans, Mari, *A Dark and Splendid Mass*, Writers & Readers Publishing Incorporated, Danbury, CT, 1992

Giovanni, Nikki, *Love Poems*, Morrow, New York, NY, 1997

Giovanni, Nikki, *RE: Creation*, Broadside Press, Detroit, MI, 1970

Giovanni, Nikki, *Blues: For All the Changes*, Morrow, New York, NY, 1999

Jackson, Angela, *And All These Roads Be Luminous: Poems Selected and New*, Northwestern University Press, Evanston, IL, 1998

Jackson, Angela, *Voodoo/Love Magic*, Third World Press, Chicago, IL, 1974

Jackson, Angela, *Dark Legs and Silk Kisses: The Beatitudes of the Spinners*, Northwestern University Press, Evanston, IL, 1993

Knight, Etheridge, *Poems from Prison: By Etheridge Knight*, Broadside Press, Detroit, MI, 1968

Knight, Etheridge, *Belly Song and Other Poems*, Broadside Press, Detroit, MI, 1973

Knight, Etheridge, *Born of a Woman: New and Selected Poems*, Houghton Mifflin, Boston, MA, 1980

Last Poets, *Vibes from the Scribes: Selected Poems*, Pluto Press, London, UK, 1985

Madhubuti, Haki, *Direction Score: Selected and New Poems*, Broadside Press, Detroit, MI, 1971

Madhabuti, Haki, *Killing Memory, Seeking Ancestors*, Lotus Press, Twin Lakes, WI, 1987

Madhabuti, Haki, *Black Pride: Poems*, Broadside Press, Detroit, MI, 1968

Madhabuti, Haki, *Heartlove: Wedding and Love Poems*, Third World Press, Chicago, IL, 1998

Neal, Larry, *Hoodoo Hollerin' Bebop Ghosts*, Howard University Press, Washington, DC, 1974

Neal, Larry, *Black Boogaloo; Notes on Black Liberation*, Journal of Black Poetry Press, San Francisco, CA, 1969

Plumpp, Sterling, *Half Black, Half Blacker*, Third World Press, Chicago, IL, 1970

Plumpp, Sterling, *The Mojo Hands Call, I Must Go*, Thunder's Mouth Press, New York, NY, 1982

Plumpp, Sterling, *Ornate With Smoke*, Third World Press, Chicago, IL, 1997

Redmond, Eugene, *The Eye in the Ceiling*, Writers & Readers Publishing, Incorporated, Danbury, CT, 1991

Redmond, Eugene, *Rivers of Bones and Flesh and Blood: Poems*, Black River Writers, Danbury, CT, 1971

Redmond, Eugene, *In a Time of Rain & Desire: New Love Poems*, Black River Writers, Danbury, CT, 1973

Rodgers, Carolyn, *How I Got Ovah: New and Selected Poems*, Anchor Press, Norwell, MA, 1975

Rodgers, Carolyn, *Songs of a Black Bird*, Third World Press, Chicago, IL, 1969

Rodgers, Carolyn, *The Heart is Ever Green: Poems*, Anchor Press, Norwell, MA, 1978

Salaam, Kalamu Ya, *The Blues Merchant: Songs (Poems) for Blkfolk*, Blkartsouth, 1969

Salaam, Kalamu Ya, *Ibura: Poetry and Fiction*, Ahidiana, New Orleans, Lousiana, 1976

Salaam, Kalamu Ya, *Icon Flowers: A Poetic Report on a Visit to Hait*, Ahidiana, 1979

Sanchez, Sonia, *Shake Loose My Skin: New and Selected Poems*, Beacon Press, Boston, MA, 1999

Sanchez, Sonia, *Does Your House Have Lions?*, Beacon Press, Boston, MA, 1998

Sanchez, Sonia, *Wounded in the House of a Friend*, Beacon Press, Boston, MA, 1997

Sanchez, Sonia, *Like the Singing Coming off the Drums: Love Poems*, Beacon Press, Boston, MA, 1998

Touré, Askia Muhammad, *Earth: For Ms. Mary Bethune and the African and Afro-American Women*, Broadside Press, 1968

Troupe, Quincy, *Transcircularities: New and Selected Poems*, Coffee House Press, Minneapolis, MN, 2002

Troupe, Quincy, *The Architecture of Language*, Coffee House Press, Minneapolis, MN, 2006

Troupe, Quincy, *Weather Reports: New and Selected Poems*, Writers & Readers Publishing Incorporated, Danbury, CT, 1991

Acknowledgments

The poems reprinted in this book were obtained and used with permission from the sources listed below. Every effort has been made to trace ownership of all copyrighted material and to secure the necessary authorization to reprint each selection. In the event of any question regarding the fair use of any materials, or any inadvertent error, the publisher will be happy to make the necessary correction in future printings.

"Ego Tripping" and "Knoxville, Tennessee" from *The Collected Poems of Nikki Giovanni Compilation* by Nikki Giovanni, copyright 2003, HarperCollins. Previously published material 1968, 1970, 1971, 1972, 1974, 1975, 1978, 1979, 1983, 1995, 1996. Used by permission of Nikki Giovanni.

"Preface to a Twenty Volume Suicide Note," "Ka'Ba," and "A Poem for Black Hearts" by Amiri Baraka. Used by permission of Amiri Baraka.

"A Song For Patriots 2/Rhythm and Blues" and "Survival: A Chant" by Askia M. Touré. Used by permission of Askia M. Touré.

"Lament" and "Inspiration" by Kalamu Ya Salaam. Used by permission of Kalamu Ya Salaam.

About the Editor

Useni Eugene Perkins is nationally recognized for writings that focus on youth and youth issues. Historian and writer Lerone Bennett, Jr. cited Perkins' book *Home Is a Dirty Street: The Social Oppressions of Black Children* as one of the most important books on the sociology of the streets since the publication of *Black Metropolis*. Other notable books by Perkins include *Harvesting New Generations: The Positive Development of Black Youth, Explosion of Chicago's Black Street Gangs: 1970 to Present,* and *Afrocentric Self-Discovery Workbook for Black Youth.* He is also publisher and editor of *Black Child Journal* and editor of *Successful Black Parenting* magazine. Perkins has authored 25 plays, including six children's musicals. In 1999 he was inducted into the International Literary Hall of Fame for Writers of African Descent.

Two Adinkra symbols are used as decorative elements in this book.

The word *adinkra* means "goodbye." Originally, Adinkra symbols were used in traditional African cultures to honor the dead. Developed by the people of Ghana and Côte d'Ivoire in West Africa, each symbol expressed the qualities attributed to the deceased. Today, Adinkra symbols are used in a variety of ways, including as design elements on contemporary clothing, interior design and in print graphics.

This symbol is called *fawohodie*.

It represents independence, freedom and emancipation.

This symbol is called *pempamsie*.

It represents readiness, steadfastness and hardiness.